DIVAN

of

LALLESHWARI

DIVAN
of
LALLESHWARI

Translation and Introduction

Paul Smith

NEW HUMANITY BOOKS
BOOK HEAVEN
Booksellers & Publishers

NEW HUMANITY BOOKS

BOOK HEAVEN

(Booksellers & Publishers for over 40 years)

47 Main Road

Campbells Creek Victoria 3451

Australia

www.newhumanitybooks.com

ISBN: 978-1724945747

Poetry/Kashmir/History/Literature/Mysticism/ Shaivism
Sufism/Bhakti

CONTENTS

The Life, Times & Poetry of Lalleshwari

Lalleshwari, Lalla Ded or Lallayogeshwari, is the famous female poet/saint and probably God-realized soul from Kashmir who lived at *exactly* the same time as the incomparable Hafiz of Shiraz (1320-1392).

Her *vakhs* (poem/sayings) are sung even today in Kashmir. Born in Pandrethan, near Srinagar, she was married at a young age but the marriage was a failure and she walked out at the age of twenty-four.

She became a disciple of Siddha Srikantha (Sed Bayu). It must have taken a lot of courage on her part to walk out of a marriage and to walk around unclothed as she did.

She was treated with contempt by some and with extreme respect and reverence by others, seeing her as a saint and eventually as God-realized.

Her *vakhs* or poem/sayings numbering around two hundred are some of the oldest examples of Kashmiri in written form that have come down to us.

She was a bridge between Hindu mysticism and Sufism. Muslims knew her as Lalla Arifa and Hindus as Lalleshwari. She is supposed to have suckled when a baby Sheikh Nurudin the Sufi mystic who was known as Nund Rishi to the Hindus of Kashmir. (See Appendix at end of book on him).

Her poems are more influential today than they have ever been, not only in Kashmir, but around the world.

Some incidents in her eventful life have been passed down to us. One day her Master or Guru was bathing in the river while just a little upstream Lalleshwari was scrubbing the outer sides of an earthen pot full of dirt. Her Master scornfully told her that the pot could never be clean if she only scrubbed the outer part. She replied, "So how can your body become pure as long as its inside isn't also cleaned?"

Often when walking about she was followed by many children who would shout at her, mocking her as youngsters do when they see a strange-looking person. She was never upset inside. On this particular day she was followed by a croed of noisy children as she passed a shop of a cloth merchant. The merchant was angry with them for teasing her and told them to leave her alone. She went over to him and asked him to give her a long piece of cloth. Immediately he went into his shop and brought out a a piece and gave it to her. She then told him to cut it exactly into halves and make sure they were of equal weight. He did this, balancing the two pieces in a scale. Then she placed on piece on one of her shoulders and the other on the other and walked off. The, a person walking past her would wave to her and she would make a knot in the piece on her left shoulder. If another person would be disrespectful to her she would make a knot onin the piece on her right shoulder. So, as she walked about she met many people and some would salute her and others be disrespectful and so she made many knots. In the evening she went back to the cloth merchant's shop and handed him the two pieces and asked him to weigh them both to see if any had gained weight. They were placed on the scale and of course balanced equally. Lalleshwari then smiled at him and said, "Why were you angry with those boys who were calling me names, Respect of disrespect makes no difference to me, just like the knots in both pieces, or both sides make no difference to this cloth!"

She once entered a temple in which her Guru *(Qutub)* was worshipping the idols. She wanted to remind him that God was present everywhere and wasn't limited to temples or places of worship. He asked her why she was there and she told him she wanted to relieve herself and being naked she had come into the temple for privacy. He quickly led her out of there saying it was a place where idols were worshipped and it would be sacrilegious to do what she intended to do in there. She asked him to show her a place where there were no idols, He took her away to another spot and she removed some of the earth and there was a buried idol. He then took her to another place and the same thing happened. She then said to him:

Idol, is just a lump of stone, temple is too:

from the top to bottom nothing but stone.

Learned teacher, what worship do you do?

Learn to control breath... your mind hone!

Many stories about her are about her miraculous powers, even when she was still with her husband...

Lalleshwari used to go out in the morning early... she crossed the river without her feet touching the water, then she sat at the *ghat* of Zinpura village where is the shrine of Natta Kesha Bhairava. After she did he ablutions she stayed in communion with God. Her suspicious husband one followed her quietly to see where she went. He thought that leaving early in the morning and sitting by the riverbank was madness... he didn't know why she did it. He became angry and after she had meditated for a while she returned with and earthen pot full of water on her head. He struck her with a stick. The pot broke into pieces but the water wasn't spilt and sat perfectly on her head. Ten she came into the house and filled all the empty pots with this water and still it wasn't all gone so she threw what remained outside the house and a pond was formed. It is said this pond still exists and is called Lalla Trag.

Valkh

The *Vakh* (like the *Sakhs* of Kabir... are four line (or two couplets) poems... usually in the form of a-b-a-b of 'sayings' that were mainly famous from the poems of our great female Sufi/Shaiva Perfect Saint Lalla Ded, the 14th century Kashmiri poet.

There have been many books and plays and music on
Lalleshwari recently

ICONS OF KASHMIR

SHIVA YOGINI LALLESHVARI

Prof. Chaman Lal Raina

Publication Division
SANJEEVANI SHARDA KENDRA
ANAND NAGAR, BOHRI, JAMMU PH : 2501480

JAISHREE K. ODIN

Lallā to Nūruddīn
Rishi-Sufi Poetry of Kashmir

A Translation and Study

naked song

lalla

LALLA-VAKYANI OR THE WISE SAYINGS OF LAL-DED - A MYSTIC POETESS OF ANCIENT KASHMIR
SIR GEORGE GRIERSON, K.C.I.E

LALLA DED

Selected Poems

Translation and Introduction

Paul Smith

NEW HUMANITY BOOKS
BOOK HEAVEN
Booksellers & Publishers

LALLA DED

Life & Poems

Translation and Introduction

Paul Smith

Introduction to Sufi Poets Series

NEW HUMANITY BOOKS

BOOK HEAVEN
Booksellers & Publishers

Mystical Verses of Lallā
A Journey of Self Realization

Translated with an Introduction
by
JAISHREE KAK

Illustrations by Joseph Singer

Word of Lalla the Prophetess

Richard Carnac Temple

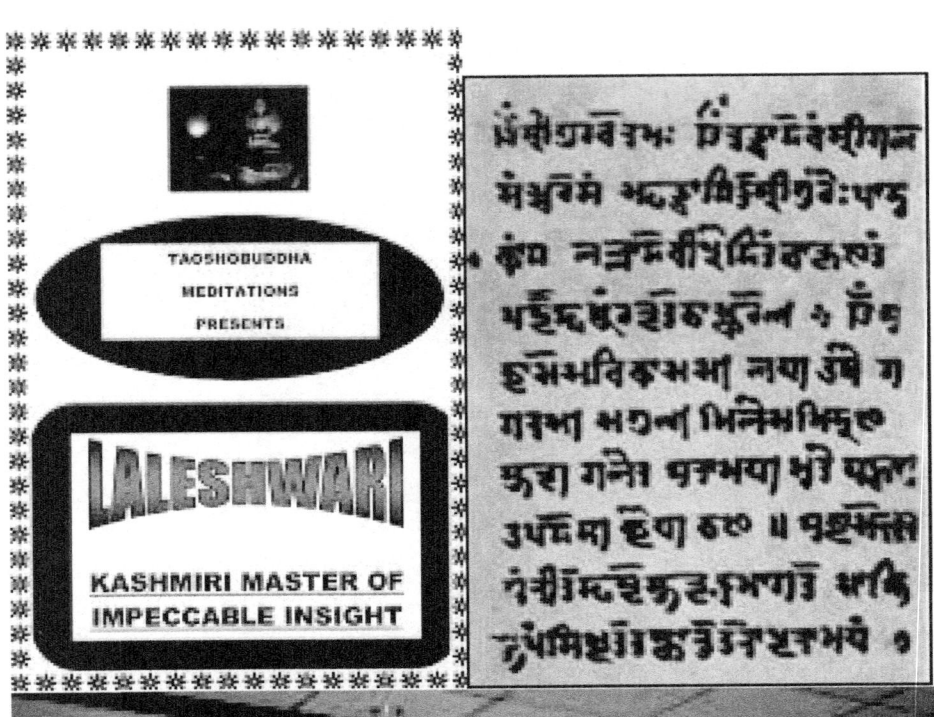

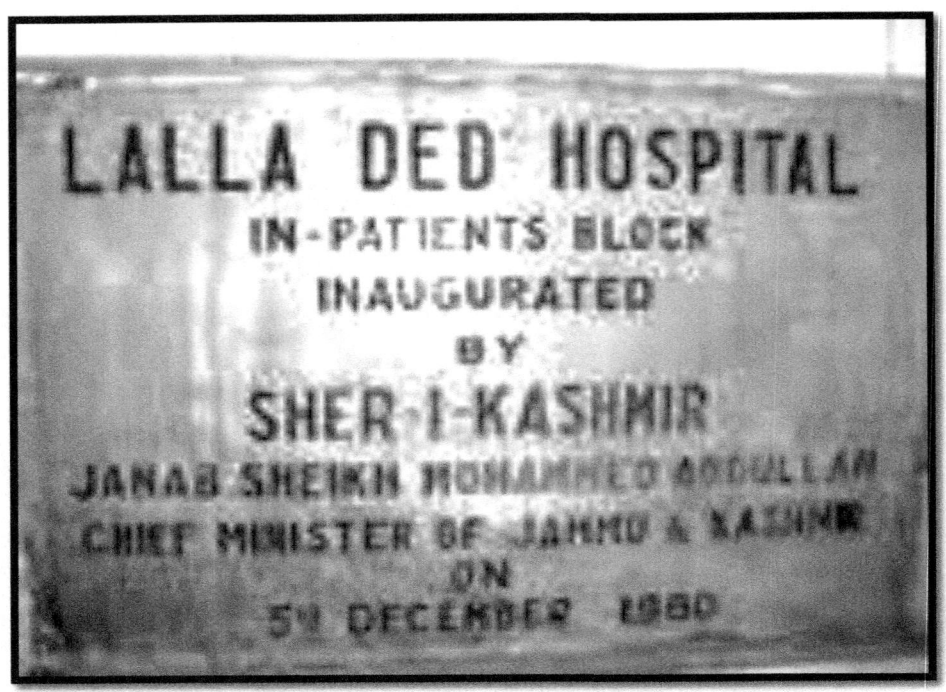

LALLA DED is a solo one act performed by Mita Vasisht. The play is a theatrical collage of poems, songs, thoughts and philosophy of the medieval poetess Lalla Ded from Kashmir. Though born to Brahmins this fiery artist transgressed all boundaries by discarding her clothes at an early age and remained unclad all her life. Her poems or vaakhs were short and pithy and they resonated secular values transcending the narrow confines of caste and religion that had crippled India in those times. Everything about LALLA DED - her life, her vaakhs, challenged dogmas and ossified perceptions. The lights of the show are by renowned Ashok Sagar Bhagat from NSD Delhi and the performance is in three languages - Hindi English and Kashmiri. The play lasts for 80 minutes. –

Writers: Meeta Vasisht, Vishnu Mathur, Rajesh Jha,
Directors: Meeta Vasisht, Vishnu Mathur.

Selected Bibliography...

Lalla Ded: Life & Poems, Translation & Introduction by Paul Smith, New Humanity Books, Campbells Creek 2014.

Lalla Ded: Selected Poems, Translation & introduction Paul Smith, New Humanity Books, Campbells Creek, 2012.

Mystical Verses of Lalla: A Journey of Self Realization, Translated with an Introduction by Jaishree Kak, Illustrations by Joseph Singer. Motilal Banarsidass Publishers, New Delhi, 2007.

Lal Ded by Jayalal Kaul, Sahitya Akademi, New Delhi, 1973.

Lalla-Vakyani: or The Wise Sayings of Lal Ded. Edited and translated by Sir George Grierson and Lionel D. Barnett, Royal Asiatic Society, London, 1920.

I Lalla: The Poems of Lal Ded, Translated by Ranjit Hoskote, Penguin Books, New Delhi, 2011.

To the Other Shore: Lalla's Life and Poetry, Jaishere Kaik Odin, Vitasta, New Delhi, 1999.

The Religion and Teachings of Lalla, by Richard Carnac Temple, Vintage Books, New Delhi, 1990.

The Wise Sayings of Laleshwari. Translated by S.N. Charagi, Trust Publishing House, Srinagar, 1938.

Sufism in Kashmir by Abdul Qaiyum Rafiqi, Bharatiya Publishing House, Delhi, 1972.

A History of Sufism in India Volume One, by Saiyid Athar Abbas Rizvi, Munshiram Manoharlal Pub. New Delhi 1978 (Pages 349-50).

Poetry of India: Translation and Introduction by Paul Smith, New Humanity Books, Campbells Creek, 2013.

Sufis & Dervishes: Their Art and Use of Poetry

It has been said that Adam was the first Sufi and Perfect Master (Qutub) and that he was also the first poet as he named everything and so through his 'Adamic Alphabet' all languages were born and so... all poetry. Two of Arabia's most highly regarded scholars of the poetic form also claim he was the father of the poetic form of the *ghazal*... the form most used by Sufi and Dervish poets up to the present day.

Sufism is said by many Masters and authors to have always existed since Adam as the esoteric side of each faith that has begun by an appearance of that original Perfect Master coming back as the Rasool, Prophet, Messiah, Avatar, Buddha, etc., whatever that Divine One is called.

Many Perfect Masters (Qutubs) were poets and many were not. Many came after the appearance of the Prophet Mohammed and many came before him. But, Sufis and Dervishes were called by those names after he passed from this world. The first 'Sufi' is probably Mohammed's son-in-law Hazrat Ali who composed one of the first *ghazals* ever recorded that essentially sums up the meaning of Sufism and Dervishness...

You do not know it, but in you is the remedy;

you cause the sickness, but this you don't see.

You are but a small form... this, you assume:

but you're larger than any universe, in reality.

You are the book that of any fallacies is clear,

in you are all letters spelling out, the mystery.

You are the Being, you're the very Being... It:

you contain That, which contained cannot be!

I have used both the terms 'Sufis' and 'Dervishes' in this book because some of poets called themselves not one but the other and criticized the other, for... during the time that they were alive, having become corrupt and following false masters. Hafiz, for instance, always called himself a Dervish and often when mentioning Sufis in his poetry it was usually to criticize them. During his lifetime in Shiraz there was an extremist Sufi Order led by a false master and Shaikh Ali Kolah who sided with various dictators and subjected the people to a very vicious brand of fundamentalism (see my biog. of Hafiz, *Hafiz of Shiraz* 3 vols. for Hafiz's almost lifelong clash with this false Sufi). By the 13th Century many Sufi Orders had become corrupt and full of various dogmas, useless rituals and power hungry and hypocritical shaikhs and false masters. Those who called themselves 'Dervishes' then really meant 'true Sufis'.

The first Sufi and Dervish poets composed in Arabic even though some of them, including the famous and infamous Sufi martyr Mansur al-Hallaj, were originally from Persia... he was from Shiraz. From the 10th to the 15th century the vast majority of Sufi and Dervish and other poets in the region composed in Persian, a few in the new languages of Turkish and Urdu and some like Kabir in Hindi and Lalla Ded in Kashmiri; after that... the languages most used by the most conscious and influential poets were Urdu, Punjabi and Sindhi, as the stream of God-consciousness moved originally from Arabia and Egypt to Iraq and Syria then into Iran and Afghanistan and Turkey and finally into the Indian Sub-Continent and Kashmir.

To follow this golden thread of Spiritual Poetry one must follow the true Spiritual Hierarchy of real Saints and God-realized Souls... Perfect Masters, their lives and stories are to be found in the many books listed below and in many others.

What is the essential belief and philosophy of the Sufi and Dervish Masters and Poets? To put it as simply as possibly... The Love of God, the belief in God in human form, the love and respect for all of God's Creation and to try to not hurt anyone or thing. And of course a belief in Truth,

Love and Beauty as the greatest of the Divine Attributes. A belief similar, if not the same as the Christian Mystics and Vedantists and believers in the inner way of most religions.

Further Reading...

A History of Ottoman Poetry by E.J.W. Gibb. Volume One, Luzac & Co. Ltd. London 1900. (Pages 33-69.)

A Critical Appreciation of Arabic Mystical Poetry by Dr. S.H. Nadeem, Adam Publishers. New Delhi, 2003.

Sufi Poems, A Mediaeval Anthology by Martin Lings, Islamic Texts Society, Cambridge, 2004.

The Way of the Mystics: The Early Christian Mystics and The Rise of the Sufis by Margaret Smith, Sheldon Press, 1976.

In the Garden of Myrtles: Studies in Early Islamic Mysticism by Tor Andrae, Translated by Birgitta Sharpe. State University of New York Press, Albany. 1987.

Muslim Saints and Mystics... Episodes from the 'Memorial of the Saints' by Farid al-Din Attar, Translated by A.J. Arberry. Routledge and Kegan Paul, London, 1966.

Kashf Al-Mahjub of Al-Hujwiri. Translated by R.A. Nicholson, Luzac, London. 1967.

Adam: The First Perfect Master & Poet by Paul Smith, New Humanity Books, Campbells Creek, 2012.

The Mystics of Islam by Reynold A. Nicholson. Routledge and Kegan Paul, London, reprint 1974.

Vakhs…

One has to endure cloudbursts and lightning,

or at noon the sudden darkness that comes…

or the body that two grindstones are crushing.

With patience, accept it, contentment comes!

In the mortar of love, my heart I

ground;

I calmed down after evil thoughts

left…

I tasted it, after it, I roasted and

burned!

By doing this, will I die… or alive be

left?

At dawn I woke, with my restless mind I called;
I withstood pain then to God I turned, saying:
"I'm Lalla, Lalla, Lalla," and woke my Beloved.
With that One, mind and body I kept purifying.

I was abused and slandered, I put up with it all:
of my past and present… scandals everywhere!
I'm Lalla: this longing of mine rose, not to fall.
My goal I attained, of nothing else was aware.

On many paths, soles of my feet I wore away:

only one path was revealing the truth to me.

Why aren't all hearing this fascinated, today?

Lalla only one word in a hundred heard clearly.

My Master, again and again I kept on asking...
"What name has that, which can't be defined?"
Such question again and again was exhausting.
Out of this nothing... something has happened!

When to this self I was firmly
attached,
from me, hidden You were still
staying.
While I was seeking You, time
passed:
looking in, You and I blissfully,
uniting!

You are the earth… You are the sky
too;
You are the night, the wind and the
day:
Sandalwood, rose, water, grain, are You.
You are… all! What to offer? Please
say!

You, Divine One, all of creation permeate:

You, Divine One, all of matter… enliven.

You, Divine One, without sound resonate!

Who, O One Divine, can know You, even?

Only one piece of advice my Master gave to me:

turn the consciousness inward... from the outer.

The initiation of Lalla became only this, for me:

that is the reason why I, naked, began to wander.

When... will you be remembering,

vow that in the womb, you made?

Die even before your body is dying,

at death you'll be at a higher grade.

I did not wait for the right time or trust in anything;

the wine that I, Lalla, was drinking, was my poetry.

I was catching the darkness inside and it gathering

and then I was ripping it into bits: now, do you see?

They can call me names, they can criticize me:

let them be calling me whatever they want to!

They can be offering to me flowers, devotedly:

I'm not impressed, so who gains... me... you?

With thirst and starvation don't hurt your body:

be taking care of your body when it is exhausted!

On your religious rites and fasts may a curse be:

the real religion's to be good to others... instead!

I came into this world, straight…

but my return was a crooked line.

Being poor by river was my fate!

To cross over, could I pay a fine?

With a loose-spun rope my boat I am towing:

I pray God hears me, brings me across safely.

Like water in unbaked clay away I'm wasting:

O God, my one desire is to get home, help me!

Mind, I weep for you, loving the illusion:
when you are dead not even a shadow on
will go of this world when you pass on…
so why have you your real Self forgotten?

A vast pit's under you, above you dance!

Sir, tell me, how you can keep doing this?

You will leave all riches... extravagance!

O sir, your meal, how can you enjoy this?

I am a wooden bow, a rush-grass arrow,

an ignorant carpenter, a palace building:

a shop unlocked in a busy bazaar... I go

on unclean... my state who is knowing?

I came from what direction, what road:

how to know road to where I'm going?

Right guidance soon lessens my load:

an empty breath's worth... is nothing!

Bag of candy's knot is loose upon my shoulder,

my burden is so heavy…

how can I now go on?

Master's words to be detached make me suffer:

a flock with no shepherd,

how can I now go on?

I saw a wise man, who was of hunger dying,

as the leaves fell with winds of near winter.

Then I saw a fool who was his cook beating,

now... Lalla waits for of world ties to sever.

When the washer-man on stone slab dashed me,

with soap and washing soda rubbing harshly…

and tailor with scissors cut me up, completely,

then, I, Lalla, the ultimate bliss did have, fully!

From me I came out seeking the moonlight,

I went on seeking what is like with the like.

O Naryana, all is You, all is Your Light...

as all is You, how can there be any 'like'? *

*Note: Naryana... the Supreme Being.

Soul is always new, the moon is ever new:

I saw the universal waters... always new!

As I, Lalla, cleaned body and mind anew,

I Lalla, am ever new, ever new, I am new!

What's happened, what's become of me?

Everything I was attached to, has gone...

all of my songs are saying, continually...

I Lalla am on a lake, where's bank, home?

I sought for my Self, but, it was
worthless,
the hidden knowledge not found,
remained.
Then in Self I was lost, nectar was
endless:
the cups were full but them no one
drained!

Put on clothes that from cold protects you,

eat enough food that you won't be hungry.

Let mind concentrate upon the Self in you:

the body as food for crows of the forest see.

Into a universe of birth and rebirth I was coming,

through asceticism's light... knowledge I gained.

Death of anyone is nothing to me as is my dying:

if I live then it's fine, and fine it is if I have died!

Although some are sleep they're really all

seeing;

although some are awake, they're seeing

nothing.

Some after a sacred bath still unclean are

staying,

and others even householders detached are

being.

My Master, just one piece of advice gave me,

stop looking outside, start to look... inwardly.

That was the one rule given to Lalla, clearly:

that is the reason naked I went for all to see!

Who is fast asleep and who is wide awake?

Out from what lake... is the water oozing?

What to God can one offer... for His sake?

What is the highest state, one is attaining?

I ground up my heart in love's mortar...

I calmed down as evil thoughts left me.

I burned it away, for I had gone too far,

now what I've done to me is a mystery!

I followed what I read, but I

realized

what I experienced... through

living!

Lion of desires into a jackal I

tamed:

I followed Truth, then was

knowing.

You are the earth, You are the heavens
too:
You're the night and the wind and the
day!
Offering, sandalwood, flowers are all
You:
You're all, so what can I offer, please
say!

As ocean of existence see your mind…

if not held in, angry words out will fly!

If on scales of Truth they are weighed,

such words weigh even less than a fly!

O restless mind, don't let fear into heart,

the One without beginning cares for you.

Hunger goes on so long once it does start:

cry only to that One to feed Word to you.

That one who can control the breath,

won't by thirst or hunger be touched.

Whoever can do this until their death

will be born a lucky one in this world.

Lord, me or other than me... I do not know:

I have only this sinful body been knowing.

That You am I and I'm You I didn't know:

"You am I and I am You," I am doubting!

Mind, why by the world are you fascinated?

Why do you believe that real is the illusory?

You're on the wrong path from being stupid:

death, rebirth, coming, going... is your story!

Embarrassment's chain will be breaking

when mocking taunts one can tolerate...

and robes of self-pity's away are burning,

if unbridled horse inside is held at gate.

To the five, ten, eleven... what will I do?*

They all came out of pot, then... departed!

If they had united, pulled on the rope too;

cow, eleventh wouldn't have misplaced.*

*Notes: The 'pot' is the physical form and the 'five' are the main experiences in the gross word; the 'ten' are the five organs of sense and the five of action and the eleven are those senses plus the mind and the 'cow' is God-consciousness.

As moonlight ended to the mad mind I called

out to the love of God to soothe its suffering...

"It is me, it is me, Lalla!" Beloved awakened!

We were one: mind and body I was purifying!

I have to put up with both the good and bad:

so my ears do not hear, eyes see nothing too.

When in heart of Self an awakening I've had,

in middle of hurricane a lamp shines through.

If a thousand abuses are hurled at me

in my heart no suffering I am feeling,

if of Sankara* I remain a true devotee.

A mirror any ashes will not be soiling.

*Note: Sankara in another name for Shiva… the pure Spirit or Soul, God in
the Beyond State or the male principle of the Godhead; Sakhti is nature, the
creative or female principle.

Self can be called Shiva, Kesava, Mahavira,

or the Buddha who is born of the lotus, too!

By whatever name it's called, that It frees a

one like me from worldly corruption, is true!

Blue-throat, You have six, I have six too!*

But without You, into affliction I will fall.

There's no difference between me and You

except I'm slave to six You're Master of all.

*Notes: Shiva is often called 'Blue-throat' or 'the blue-throated One'. The six attributes of humans are anger, bewilderment, passion, arrogance, avarice and jealousy. The six attributes of God are omniscience, contentment, knowledge, power, bliss, omnipotence.

I was abused and I was slandered daily,

scandals about my past and present too!

I'm Lalla, my longing never leaves me...

winning my desire, I was unaffected too.

I desired no riches from the life I led,

luxuries and greed were not for me…

I ate sufficient and poverty suffered:

to God I was devoted, passionately!

Over and over my Master I asked…

"What's the name of the nameless?"

I became exhausted by my asking…

out of nothing came more than less!

I, Lalla, got tired from seeking that

One:

beyond myself I sought, even beyond

me!

I saw bolts on door as I sought that

One:

my gaze became fixed, that One I did

see!

I locked the doors and windows of my body,

caught, controlled thief of my vital energy.

Inside closet of my heart I tied it tightly…

with the sound of *Om* I whipped it fiercely!

Steed of my mind I held with the rein,

I learnt to control breath by practice...

The orb of moon melted into my vein: *

this nothing went, into Nothingness!

*Note: "Orb of the moon' in yoga is the seventh chakra.

Into the *Om* sound I became absorbed,

like coal... I burned my false self away!

I left all six planes and seventh gained:

then illuminated was Lalla, this I say!*

*Note: By far the best explanation of the seven planes or 'paths' of conscious
can be found in 'God Speaks: The Theme of Creation & Its Purpose' by
Meher Baba, Dodd, Mead and Company New York 1955.

Moonlight came when sun disappeared:
moon went, consciousness was staying.
When mind left only nothingness stayed:
form, soul and universe were all leaving!

You stayed hidden away from me,

when to my false self I was glued!

When finally my real Self I did see

in ecstasy You and I were United!

Going on through the nothingness alone...

I, Lalla, of myself all consciousness let go:

When the secret I found of my inner One,

in the mud for Lalla a lotus did then grow.

On many paths soles of my feet wore away,

the true path was shown to me by just one.

Why don't all hearing me fall in love today?

In a hundred words I, Lalla, heard just one!

In a moment, I saw a river, flowing…

in a moment not one bridge did

I see.

In a moment a shrub, roses blooming:

in a moment, no thorns, roses…

I see!

I, Lalla, set out full of deep longing…
day and night I searched everywhere.
In my house a wise man I was seeing,
I held onto him… my luck, was there!

The works I did became worshipping,

whatever I said was a sacred *mantra*.

In my body all of this was happening:

Shiva does this, this is His Formula!

From my soul impurities I burnt up:

in my heart, all desires I murdered!

Then my name of Lalla, all took up,

when I sat there: I had surrendered!

Eating, eating, eating nowhere takes
you:
but, if you stop eating you become
proud!
Eat in moderation… balanced will be
you:
moderation opens doors... that are
closed.

Stopping a stream or fire that's raging,

or being able to levitate into the sky...

a wooden cow to be able to be milking,

in the end is nothing but deceit, say I!

As time passes and your desires go, too,

choose to be a recluse... or a householder.

You will know God is pure and in all too:

you'll become of what you are a beholder.

One knowing self and others as equal,

the night and the day as the same too;

one who frees mind of all that is dual,

sees the Supreme Master... the True!

For actions, one must take responsibility...
many others will all their fruits be sharing.
I offer all actions to the Supreme Divinity:
then it's fine with me wherever I'm going!

Shiva, is in everyone and everything:

Hindus and Muslims are the same…

be wise and your real Self be knowing,

with the Master that's your real game.

Anyone who the Master's words are trusting,

with reins of wisdom mind's steed holds back;

anyone gains bliss who senses are controlling:

who's dying, who killed and won't come back?

One who kills thieves... pride, lust,

greed,

then in all humility, the people is

serving...

has found the Divine Master by this

deed,

and knows all else as ashes...

everything!

One calling Shiva's name, on *hamsa* meditating,

and every day and night does all worldly duties;

frees mind from duality, not of reward thinking,

Supreme Master will grace as that one pleases. *

*Note: Hamsa, meaning 'swan' is a meditation in the Saiva tradition meaning the Unity of the lover and the beloved.

I didn't wait for the moment, not trusting it,
what I Lalla, drank, was wine of my poetry!
Then, I seized the inner darkness, grabbed it
and brought it down... into shreds I ripped it!

There, there are no words, thoughts, here, there:
one does not enter by vows of silence or yoga…
also, Shiva and Sakti are not dwelling… There;
that 'Supreme Divinity' seek, that… Treasure!

Some give up home, some the monastery,

but if mind isn't controlled, it's fruitless!

Day and night all breaths count, exactly,

and where you are stay: do less than less!

Kus-grass, flowers, seeds, water... all useless,

for one who the Master's words are accepting.

Longing, one will on Shiva meditate, no less...

absorbed in joy, free, that one is not returning.

I Lalla, went hoping to bloom like cotton-flower:

the carder and cleaner gave many a blow, to me.

From wheel, gossamer of me made the spinner...

and, in weaver's workroom I was hung brutally.

O Master, You are same as God to me…

reveal the inner meaning, that You know!

Two breaths from naval rise undoubtedly:

why's *huh* cold, *hah* hot? I want to know.*

"Region of the naval is by nature fiery,

so air rises up your throat, out as *hah!*

it meets river from Head, suddenly...

so *hah* is hot and Head's cold is *huh!**

*Note: Head = Brahma-randhra.

I looked outside although it was within:

my insides, were by my breath soothed.

God and world are one I found within...

the inner and the outer, became merged.

Slowly, slowly, breath in throat I controlled,

the lamp shone and my real nature was seen.

That light that was inside me I then realized,

in the darkness I then seized it, held it, clean.

Put upon yourself the garment of knowledge:
on your heart couplets of Lalla write, no less.
Meditating upon *Om,* Lalla was absorbed...
fear of death went as arrived Consciousness.

All, knowing Light, Consciousness, Bliss,

while still alive they have been liberated...

but tangled up in the nets of more births is

all foolish ones, adding knots by a hundred.

Suddenly, I saw a cooking hearth blazing:

suddenly, I could see no smoke or fire, too.

Suddenly Pandavas' mother I was seeing;

suddenly, I saw aunt in potter's hut, too. *

*Note: The Pandavas, the famous heroes of the Mahabharata, were kings, and their mother, Kunti, was queen. Yet through treachery they were all at one time reduced to misery and wandered hungry and thirsty until they came to the city of King Drupada. With their mother the Pandavas disguised as mendicant Brahmans, found refuge in the hut of a potter. Lalla adds that the potter's wife or her children saw Kunti as an aunt.

Who is asleep and who awake?

What lake keeps oozing away?

What offering, will God take?

In what Station will one stay?

Mind is asleep and the soul is awake:
five organs are the lake, oozing away!
The self is the offering God will take:
Shiva consciousness, is State to stay!

Over the sky the steed of mind's wandering;

thousands of miles, in the twinkle of an eye!

The wise one in and out breath is controlling

by the bridle of Self-Realization; this, say I.

Through practice the creation will disappear,
into the Nothing all worlds will be merging.
When Nothing goes Everything will appear:
my dear teacher, this… is the true teaching!

Day passes and night is arriving,

up to the sky the earth's reaching.

Eclipse, new moon is swallowing:

knowledge, is Shiva worshipping.

Controlling breath, through six forests I cut again

until the moon woke me, material world I gave up.

I roasted heart in love's fire as one roasts grain...

at that moment I found Sankara, when I gave up!*

*Note: The six forests are the six chakras or energy centres.
Sankara is Shiva... the Godhead.

When will you the vow be remembering
that in your mother's womb you made.
Kind sir, die even before you are dying,
by dying you will reach a higher grade.

How often I drank wine, that Sindhu-water,

how often another part upon stage I played,

how often of a piece of flesh I was an eater...

I remain Lalla... in what way did it me alter?

Humankind, why do you twist a rope of
sand?
With such a line the boat won't move for
you!
What fate God wrote for you on time's
sand,
dear, none can change... it will come, to
you!

Mind isn't eased through clothes or eating,

goal is attained by false hopes giving away.

Fear of death is from the scriptures reading,

one not leaning on them finds peace one day!

She gives milk to baby as a mother,

that one has another role as a wife,

then as *maya* she acts as deceiver:*

hear, Shiva isn't easy: it's your life!

*Note Maya is the illusion, the material world.

Listen, the bitter is often the sweet,
the sweet's often what is poisonous.
When hard work and devotion meet
the final goal is more closer... for us.

We come and go, and come and still go…
we move on, and on… day and night too.
Where we come from… back we must go:
it's something? That it's nothing is true!

I remember a lake three times overflowing,

and seeing in the sky a stone… like a dish.

Harmukh to Kausar, bridge I was seeing.*

Seven times I saw world into void vanish.

*Harmukh is a mountain in Kashmir and Kausar is a
stream in Paradise.

While lost, the sense of loss I was losing:

after I was lost, I found I was in this sea.

Playing, laughing, God I was becoming...

largest part of me became this philosophy.

Idol, is just a lump of stone, temple is

too:

from the top to bottom nothing but

stone.

Learned teacher, what worship do you

do?

Learn to control breath… your mind

hone!

Why do you drown in this world of illusion?

You destroyed high road now you're in mire!

Death takes you when your time does come:

you from the fear of death, who can inspire?

Ascetic wanders from holy place to another,

seeking his real Self away from where he is!

Soul, study your Self don't be an unbeliever.

The grass looks greener the further off it is!

One wielding a sword a kingdom can gain,

and one charitable and sorry gets paradise.

One from Master, Knowledge can obtain:

one reaps fruit of actions... virtue, or vice!

If I'd known how to inner passages control,

how to cut, bind up… how to crush sorrow,

then I'd have finally the Elixir made, whole:

Shiva's hard to find, hear my advice, follow!

Bringing flowers... who is the male and woman?

What flowers should be offered for worshipping?

What kind of water to over the image pour again?

What kind of prayer, will Shiva be ever hearing?

Mind is man, desire woman flowers bringing:
offer flowers of devotion to God... in worship!
Nectar of moon for that One, be anointing…
the Shiva within will awaken... nothing to it!

Kill all desires, and on your Self meditate...
stop fantasizing for Realization has a price!
Still, it is close to you, don't far off seek it:
in nothingness is Nothing... what a prize!

Rock on some pedestal or a pavement

is the same as any that upon earth is!

Yet the same rock may a mill cement:

to get to Shiva is hard, my advice, is!

You cut hide, for yourself, pegged it:

why produce such fruit, seed to sow?

To tell a fool is throwing stones at it

that if fed; to bull, would be mellow!

Don't let ass* loose to stray from your hand,

or it's sure it will eat your neighbours saffron:

who will then offer his back, to mount… and,

where is the sword that strikes… your form?

*Note: Ass or donkey… is the mind.

The path of knowledge is like some herb garden,

enclose it with good deeds, peace, self-restraint.

Offer as sacrifice to goddess each former action:

by eating from garden they'll be cleared of taint.

Even with a kingdom, you will not be happy...
even if you renounce it, happy you're not being.
The soul that's free of desire will live eternally:
real knowledge is dead to desires, while living.

Kill lust, desire, anger those demons, deadly:
or... with their arrows, they will murder you!
Calm them with good thoughts, tranquillity...
then how unstable they are will be known too.

Focus all thoughts on path of immortality,

if mind leaves path it will become a loser.

Do not be fearful there, be calm, brave be;

a suckling baby is quiet, on lap of mother.

A fly-whisk, sunshade, chariot, throne too...

a joyful party, soft bed, pleasures of theatre:

of all of these, which will be lasting for you?

Can they take away the fear of death, ever?

Once you were a swan... now you are mute:

off with something of yours was... someone.

When mill stopped blocked was grain chute:

the miller ran off with the grain! What fun!*

God laughs, sneezes, coughs, yawns

too,

and God it is that bathes in holy

places!

God is the naked ascetic and all year

too:

recognize God is near to you, in all

faces!

I found the one path after on ten wandering…

I entered the Nothing through breath control,

I saw Shiva in all: six and three I was closing[*]

and I discovered, that Shiva was there, in all!

[*]Note: The six are the five organs of sense plus the mind.
The three are the opening in the body.

God, You all creation on earth pervade:

God, You life to all matter are giving...

God, You without any sound resonate:

God, You... who can be understanding?

My tongue was sore by reading, reciting:

practice right for You I never discovered.

Thumb, finger, I hurt from beads turning:

confusion in my mind never disappeared.

"We were in the past, in future will be:

through all the ages We were existing."

Shiva destroys, creates continuously...

like the sun goes on setting, and rising!

Shiva's the horse and Vishnu the saddle
is,
and upon the stirrup Brahma is the
rider...
through the practice of yoga the real yogi
is
recognizing the One Who alone is the
rider.

Original Sound, that is in the Nothing,

that has no colour, form, past or name...

that from self-reflection is in everything,

only that is God riding horse, the same!

Who can stop icicles dripping...

who can in one's palm hold air?

Who five senses is controlling,

in darkness the sun sees, clear!

No you, I, contemplation, contemplated:

only the Creator Who became forgetful!

No meaning in this see who are blinded,

but... seeing the One they were blissful!

Into ice or snow the cold will turn water...

these three things are not really different.

Sun of Consciousness shines, they alter

and are one... Shiva! All, is not different!

Name and integrity are water in a basket!

The mighty one who can hold air in a fist

or with hair of head an elephant tie tight,

only such a one as this will come in first!

As if from a mirror mind's filth was wiped,

and then knowledge of my Self I did gain.

The One was close when the One I spied:

that One's all, I'm nothing; not one grain!

I, Lalla, went through door of soul's garden,
and there I did see Shiva and Sakti, united.
There I was in nectar of bliss drowned when
I died while still living! I'm now not worried.

Put up with thunder and lightning,

put up with at noon the darkness...

and through grinding mill passing!

If content God comes... no stress!

APPENDIX...

Life & Times & Poetry of Nund Rishi.

Nund Rishi or Shaikh Nur ud-din, as he was afterwards named by Mir Muhammad of Hamadan, was born at Kaimuh, a village two miles to the west of Bijbihara in Kashmir in 1377. His father's name was Salar Sanz, whose ancestors were descended from the Rajas of Kishtwar in Jammu and had immigrated into Kashmir. They had been granted a *jagir* (land grant) by the then king of Kashmir, at Rupawan, a village five miles to the north-west of Tsrar, where they had settled.

Drupada Sanz was a descendant of this family and was a respectable man held in high esteem by the Kashmir Darbar. His son's name was Sul Sanz, who lived at Guda Suth village and became a disciple of a hermit named Yasman Rishi, being converted by him to Islam under the name of Salar Din. He used to take his preceptor's cows to the fields for grazing and after sometime Yasman Rishi arranged his marriage with Sadr Maji at Kaimub village.

Sadr Maji had previously lived at village Khayah in the Adven Pargana. She was a descendant of a Rajput family and as her parents had died when she was yet a child she had been adopted by a Muslim. When grown up, she had been married to a Dum at Kaimuh, by whom she had two sons named Shishu and Gandharv. After a while her husband died.

It is said that one day Salar Din together with his bride went to his religious preceptor Yasman Rishi, who was at the time sitting by a spring. The female poet Lallaeshwari (1320-1390) happened to arrive there carrying a bouquet in her hand. Yasman Rishi took it from her and gave it to Sadr Maji to smell and the same night she conceived. After the due period had elapsed, she gave birth to a son whom she named Nund Rishi. Another version is that one night a Brahman at Kaimuh village told his wife that if she rose up very early the following morning and went to the stream passing by the village, she would observe two bouquets, one of *hi* (white jasmine) and the second of *arni* (yellow jasmine) floating down and if she caught and smelt the former she would conceive and give birth in due course to a boy who would become a very holy man: but if she picked up the latter she would conceive and give birth to a boy who would also become a holy man, though not equal to the boy born of the woman who might smell the white jasmine. Sul Sanz, who was going on his night round at the time, overheard this conversation. On his return he spoke about it to his wife Sadr and enjoined on her to checkmate the Brahman's wife by going very early in the morning to the stream and catching the bouquet of white jasmine that would float down first and smelling it. She did so and succeeded in picking up the bouquet that she smelt. The Brahman's wife reached the stream later on and caught the second bouquet, which she smelt. The result was that Sadr Maji gave birth to Nund Rishi and the Brahman's wife to a boy who was named Bhum Sadhu and became a holy man performing austere penances in a cave at Bhumzu about a mile to the north of Mattan village.

When Nund Rishi was born he would not suckle his mother. The great female Sufi poet of Kashmir Lalleshwari came again and approached the new-born baby, saying to him, "You were not ashamed of being born, why then of suckling?" Hearing these words he began to suckle at once. Lalla Ded then enquired the name of the worthy mother of this worthy son and when told that it was Sadr (ocean), she remarked: "Pearls do only come out of the ocean."

When Nund Rishi grew to manhood his step-brothers named Shishu and Gandharv who were thieves, took him one night with them to help in a theft. They reached a village where they broke through the wall of a house and told Nund

Rishi to enter and bring out anything he found heavy in weight. Nund Rishi entered and found a box full of gold and silver, but he reflected that if he brought it out he would be committing a sin. So, instead of this box he brought out a stone pestle and gave it to his brothers telling them that he could find nothing heavier in the house. His brothers were angry at his stupidity in not understanding that heavy things meant precious metals and thinking that he could not understand what they actually meant, told him to bring out anything light in weight. He re-entered, and he brought out a sieve and a winnowing fan and told his brothers that there were no lighter things in the house. His brothers, disappointed at his foolishness, afterwards themselves stole a cow and handed her over to him to drive to their home, they themselves going to some other place to steal. Nund Rishi was driving the cow when he heard a dog barking wow- wow. In the Kashmiri language wow, wow means 'sow, sow.' He reflected that the dogs were reminding him of the fact that what he sowed now he would reap hereafter and that it meant that he would be punished by God for this theft. He therefore let the cow go and went home. When his brothers returned, finding that he had nut brought the cow, they asked him why he had not done so. He replied to them as follows...

The dog is barking in the yard,

brothers, give ear, listen now...

'As one sows, it'll be back hard:

you, Nund... sow, sow, sow.'

His brothers would not listen to his advice but gave him a thrashing instead for his carelessness.

He did not mind this, and said...

Who kill lust, anger, grief's snake

they will bear all with resignation.

Who seeks the One, ease take...

all as ashes in this world is seen.

In those days there lived also a female hermit named Sham Ded, who roamed about the country. She came to Nund Rishi and talked with him on the maltreatment accorded to him by his thieving brothers and said:

"A spring has been lost in the stream;

a saint has been lost among the thieves.

A deep man lost in house of fools has been:

a swan has been lost among the crows.

Another night his step-brothers again took Nund Rishi with them for the purpose of stealing and went to a house in Khudaven village that they made him enter. The owners happened to be awake and suspecting it was a thief who had entered they spoke to one another, lamenting that they were very poor... so poor as not to possess even a quilt to protect themselves from the cold of winter... so that a thief could get nothing from their house. Nund Rishi overheard them and felt pity for their poverty. He then flung his own blanket over them and came out empty-handed. His step-brothers asked him what he had secured and where his own blanket was. He replied:

I found poor people naked at Khudaven;

and so I hung my blanket to cover them!

His step-brothers were now convinced that he was a simpleton and quite unfit to join them and they told his mother that as he could not learn the art of stealing he should be given some other work. His mother told him that, since he disliked theft he might earn his livelihood by some handicraft. He replied that he would gladly comply with her wishes. She then took him to a weaver to be taught the art of weaving and was accepted as an apprentice. When his mother was gone. Nund Rishi asked the weaver why he was always alternately raising and lowering his feet. He replied that he was raising the warp in order to put in the woof; but Nund Rishi explained that this movement had another meaning saying: "When you raise your right foot it is a hint that we were dust and God raised us to life. When you lower your left foot, it indicates that we shall return to dust!" Nund Rishi next inquired: "Why have these threads been put together: what is the piece of wood that is shot to and fro in the loom; what are the threads attached to it; and what the board which you are pulling towards yourself The weaver replied that they were warp, shuttle and woof and press-board respectively. Nund Rishi replied: "No... the woof indicates that the world is an inn having two doors... by one we enter and by the other we leave. The shuttle is man and the thread in its mouth is his daily bread apportioned to him by fate; so long as it lasts he moves about in this world and when finished he is kept out like the shuttle. The board, which, when you pull it towards you to press home the woof, makes a sound like *dag dag* and indicates that our desires are killing us." The weaver got perplexed on hearing this philosophy and thought the apprentice's mind was wandering. He sent for Nund Rishi's mother and told her that her son seemed to have no inclination to learn weaving as he was not attending to the work but simply boring him with abstruse philosophical remarks and hampering him in his own work. The mother in despair took her son, telling him that as he was not inclined to work he might go away and do whatever he liked.

Nund Rishi now left to himself, dug out a cave at Kaimuh in which he began to perform austere penances. One day his mother went to see him and finding him squatting, covered with a coarse quilt, in a dark cave infested with rats, she burst into tears. Nund Rishi condoled her saying that he was extremely happy and added...

The cave seems to me to be a celestial home;

the quilt seems to me to be a silken garment.

I play with rats as if creatures of good omen.

One year seems to me to be one hour spent.

One day Nund Rishi, coming out of his cave saw some folk going about happily in party dresses and inquired what the occasion was that made the people so merry. He was told that it was the New Year's day. Thinking it an auspicious occasion, Nund Rishi began to fast from this day. His mother, coming to know of this, went to him and cried out sobbing that he had already left his home, his wife and children, and now he had left off eating and drinking: so how could he live. Nund Rishi replied: "Those who cause cattle to sweat in spring shall see ears of corn bending in autumn. If they did not toil, how could the soil have been prepared?" He meant by this that if in the vigour of youth one did not turn towards God how could one do so in sedate old age?

While Nund Rishi was performing penances in the cave, his wife, Zai Ded, together with her two sons and one daughter, came to see him and began to weep. He told her to return home and take care of her children, but she said she could not leave him. He then explained that as he had renounced the world he wanted to be left alone in the cave, where there was only dust and thorns. He said: "Desire is like the knotted wood of the forest, it can't be made into planks; beams or into cradles. He who cut and felled it will burn it into ashes."

Zai Ded then asked him what she should do with the children. He told her to take them home for that night. She obeyed. At night they all slept but in the morning they were found dead. The poor mother wept and beat her breast. When Nund Rishi came to know of this, he grieved and said:

I, a fool, erred from the beginning;

why didn't I earn money for them?

Now brass is my golden earring!

I'm son to father; me I have none!

What use warmth and fire having?

Against time I couldn't have won!

All of my flock now is scattering!

I'm son to father; me I have none!

Nund Rishi, however, thanked God that He had freed him from anxiety about the children. Zai Ded also, finding all her family ties severed, renounced the world and became a female hermit. When she died she was buried at Kaimuh village.

Nund Rishi dwelt in this cave for about twelve years, eating nothing except endive and *upalhak*.

Once his mother, Sadr Maji visited him and asked him sorrowfully how he was living on these bitter herbs. He replied:

The taste of upalhdk and of endive...
that taste is as Soma juice reckoned.
He who, leaving milk, churns water,
he so to speak, came not in this world.
Who considers others, himself equal:
he has crossed the River of the world.

Once Nund Rishi was going on an excursion towards Veri Nag. He reached a village called Hillar, near Achhabal, where he found a man performing penances in the hollow of a tree that he had himself dug out. Nund Rishi frowned at him for cutting a hole for himself in the trunk of the tree, thus spoiling it. He told him that he ought to have lived in a cave instead. He inquired of him his name and his profession. The weaver replied that his name was Suzan (meaning a 'good person) and his profession was weaving cloth. Nund Rishi addressed him with:

You'll sit at the loom and the bronze ring;

I shall tell you to listen, then you will not.

I went about, found a weaver wrong doing.

Who gave you Suzan, named you that lot?

One day Nund Rishi was sitting at the shop of a certain Musa Wani when a man came to the shop with a piece of cloth for sale. The shopkeeper told him that it was no good and, after some wrangling, gave him a very low price for it. A short time after another man came to the shopkeeper and asked if he had any cloth for sale. The shopkeeper told him that he had a piece of very good cloth, and brought out that same piece from a pot in which he had placed it, and gave it to the customer, after taking a high price for it. Nund Rishi then said to the shopkeeper that he would like to be kept in the pot so that his value might also rise, like that of the piece of cloth. This remark had such a powerful effect upon the shopkeeper that he left his business and became one of the Rishi's disciples. Nund Rishi then remarked: "God, You were pleased with Musa Wani the deceitful. Grant to me such a boon."

There was a rich man living at Drayigam a village 8 miles from Srinagar on the way to Tsrar, whose name was Sangi Ganai. He had a large number of cows. Nund Rishi once saw Sangi Ganar's wife milking her cows. There was a milk cow that she did not milk because it was very wild and would not allow anyone to milk it. Nund Rishi told her to approach this cow in his presence and milk it. The woman obeyed, though in dread of being kicked. But the animal remained quiet and allowed itself to be milked. Thenceforth the milk of this cow used to be sent every evening to Nund Rishi for his use. One day Sangi Ganai together with his family had gone somewhere, and his daughter was left in the house to take the usual supply of milk to Nund Rishi in the evening. She took him the milk, which he drank. She saw some angel-like beings sitting around him. He advised her not to speak about this vision to anybody. She returned home, but when her parents came, she disclosed this secret to them. She died soon after. The parents grieved long for her, thinking that she might not have died had she not gone with milk to Nund Rishi. The mother then stopped sending milk to him. One day she made a false excuse that a guest had come, to whom the milk was given; another day, that a cat had drunk it; and another day, that the calf had got loose and had sucked all the milk from the cow. Nund Rishi then remarked...

Calf, guest and cat were the excuse,

for three days they were enumerated.

Sin will therefore on me hang a noose

I will forget thinking of that Beloved.

May inflammation stop the desires!

If returns in a noose they will be held.

I'll bolt the door firmly if away it runs...

this body with a thorn won't be pricked.

Nund Rishi then left Drayigam village. When he had gone about 20 furlongs past Anzbur, Sangi Ganai, together with several others, went after him and requested him to return; but Nund Rishi would not go back.

A man named Manak once came to Nund Rishi and began to reproach him for his being illiterate. Nund Rishi pleaded guilty, declaring that he had really wasted his life in ignorance and that he had, therefore, become a recluse, repenting for his sins. He remarked...

The nightingale is roaming in the garden:

in empty buildings owl goes here, there...

in wilderness lion and jackal roam again:

in shit and dirt donkey looks, for a share.

"But one should not preach sermons to others and himself practise otherwise," said Nund Rishi

Once when a number of men were going to the hills they chanced to meet Nund Rishi. The latter asked them where they were going and what they were carrying. They told him that they were going towards the meadows to give salt to their flocks and were carrying provisions for themselves for a few days. He told them that they should also carry a large stock of provisions for the next world, where they would have to remain not only for a few days but for very long time. This hint stung one of them to the quick and he fainted. When he came to himself again he fell at the feet of Nund Rishi and from then on became a recluse. Nund Rishi remarked...

The conch shell is sounded by a little blowing, domes resound by beating on the kettle-drum.
Good people understand by a little hinting, wicked will not understand by beat of drum.

One day Nund Rishi went to a village and saw a worker oppressing the inhabitants. He became angry and asked the peasant why he was troubling the people and not fearing God. The worker replied that he was simply carrying out the orders of his master, who paid him. Nund Rishi smiled and remarked...

The Lord who sent us into the world,

to God we showed only indifference,

God gave us a Turkish steed to ride:

riding it we assumed the heroes' airs.

We will all be to that One devoted...

Who deaf and dumb we thought was.

The peasant, on hearing this advice, repented and from then on desisted from troubling anyone.

A farmer named Sung once came to Nund Rishi and told him that he was dissatisfied with his past deeds and wanted to renounce the world and become one of his followers. Nund Rishi directed a disciple of his named Mung to make over to Sung the duties he was performing. For some time Sung performed these duties, and then took leave to go home to see his own family. At home his family were so pleased to have him back to live with them that they would not let him return to Nund Rishi. A long time went by. Nund Rishi remembered him, saying:

Sung came and heart was glad...

so we kept him in Mung's place.

We thought he'd become gold...

outweighing all in time or space.

If it was a horse that we'd had

we'd have tied him up someplace

He's not even an ass, no steed;

he will spend at home his days.

When Sung heard that Nund Rishi was thinking him he left his home and returned to his guide to whom he remained devoted until his death.

A number of men once came to see Nund Rishi and hinted at his belonging to a low caste. Nund Rishi said...

A flower-seller's dyul is of a birth, low,

neither pony, cattle, nor cow will eat it.

When it upon head of the king does go

what happened to that low birth of it?

Nund Rishi was once going through a forest where he saw a number of men pretending to meditate on God but living an easy life and having no real love for God. He rebuked them in the following words...

People of this age to be rishis they pretend

like a prostitute when she sings of morality.

To be innocent and so gentle they pretend;

they won't sow beans, cotton-seeds... any!

They'll pass thieves in way to cheat, spend;

to hide themselves... in a forest they will be.

He further attacked hypocrisy in these following words...

By bowing down you'll not become a Rishi...

pounder in rice-mill didn't ever raise up head.

By entering a cave, God attained cannot be...

mongoose and rat never out of holes lift head.

By bathing, mind won't get clean, obviously:

the fish and otter... never any bank ascended.

If God were pleased by fasting one would see

the destitute had never food in the pot cooked!

Once Nund Rishi saw a hypocritical mullah at a mosque twirling a rosary in his hand, who took six platefuls of rice, which were brought to him by six different persons at different times, to each of whom he said he had no food at all that day. Nund Rishi then rebuked him with these words...

Your rosary to a snake could be likened:

you bend it upon seeing those disciples.

You've eaten six platefuls, to the end...

if you art a mullah then who're robbers?

In regard to dislikes, which man or beast naturally have, Nund Rishi remarked...

Pony, ass, calf are disliked by vegetable grower.

fleshy matter in the palate by a calf is disliked.

Guest is disliked by the vile wretch, a watcher:

husband's sister by daughter-in-law is disliked.

Applicable of the proclivities of one's family members Nund Rishi said...

A daughter is like an axe to a deodar forest...

it will fell it to many heaps of logs be making.

Son is like an Arabian colt in the world, next:

you can put a saddle on him and go off riding.

A brother is like a fruit tree to a the luckiest...

when there is a need it will help be providing.

Wife is like a quilt that in a basket does nest:

it will be of use in the winter or out walking.

On the vicissitudes of life, Nund Rishi once lamented with...

Tigers go back in caves, jackals are howling:

large house falls down, little house is lit up!

The poor come together, the king's worrying:

while sheep in the open graze, cooks give up!

Nund Rishi advised seeking good company and shunning the bad, contrasting the two in forcible terms. He shows that the rogue will wrong the good, attacking him with crooked words, if he is not careful...

Spend all your days with the good,

for the finest rice will get pounded.

Never go about with the wicked...

don't go near pots, soot covered!

On man's attempts to secure worldly objects, which of course result in disappointment, Nund Rishi observed...

I cast off gold and hankered after brass;

I broke a sword and made a sickle of it.

Day began to end, I lit fire but in haste,

the flame went out, pots were not on it.

In regard to the imperative necessity of devotion to God, Nund Rishi stated...

There is a moment for coming and for going...

a moment I want for devotion, O my Master!

I can't reach, this arm can't You be reaching...

I have faith in You that You I am really being.

Once Nund Rishi spoke about the futility of performing prayer without concentrating the mind on God...

If you'll hear the truth... subdue the five senses,

if you do only the body, it will not you be saving.

If you try for union with Who divinity dispenses

only then, O Rishi Mali, will prayer be working.

In regard to natural disabilities, Nund Rishi once said:

No use to a walnut break, is one toothless:

no use, has a cripple for a bow and arrow...

no use has the dog for any pearl necklaces:

no use a blind man, to lovely woman know.

Come good, come evil, there is an end, was the subject on which Nund Rishi once spoke to his favourite disciple, Nasar Baba, as follows:

When the body was bared to the wind of the Jehlam, that day has passed, O Nasar.

When we had thin curry, unsalted vegetables only to eat, that day has passed, O Nasar.

When wife was near and warm clothing covered the bed, that day has passed, O Nasar.

When boiled rice and sliced fish were provided for us, that day has passed. O Nasar.

Nund Rishi breathed his last at Rupawan village on the 26th of December 1438 at the age of 61 years. His body was carried to Tsrar and was buried on the mound called Nafla Teng. His funeral was attended by thousands of people, among whom was the then king of Kashmir, Zainu'l-abidin.

One of the biggest events that occurred in Nund Rishi's childhood was the coming of another Sufi master, Shah Hamadan to Kashmir in September 1372, 1379 and the third time in the year 1383.

Nund Rishi's life has impressed the Kashmiri people. The Afghan governor, Ata Muhammad Khan, gave, as it were, expression to public sentiment when coins were struck by him in the poet's name in 1808-10.

The University of Kashmir has honoured him by creating a Chair in his name.

The shrine of Nund Rishi in addition to the structure itself, comprises attached *Khanqah* (Sufi meeting hall), inns for the pilgrims is a place of pilgrimage for Kashmiris of all communities. The shrine contained 600-year-old handmade Persian and Kashmiri carpets, ancient objects and scrolls, some antique copies of the Koran extremely precious cut-glass chandeliers etc., all which were reduced to smoke and ashes during a fire fight between the Indian army and militants on April 11, 1995. The shrine has been rebuilt.

The Rishi order of Kashmir is a Sufi tradition associated with religious harmony it was founded by Nund Rishi. Many of the saints held dear by Kashmiris to this day were Sufi Rishis. The Rishi order has made an important contribution to the ethnic, national, social and cultural consciousness of the Kashmiri people, as well as a distinctive contribution to global Islam.

The 17th-century poet Baba Nasib sums up the impact of the Rishi order: "The candle of religion is lit by the Rishis, they are the pioneers of the path of belief. The heart-warming quality of humble souls emanates from the inner purity of the hearts of the Rishis. This vale of Kashmir, that you call a paradise, owes a lot of its charm to the traditions set in vogue by the Rishis."

The original Rishi Sufis were focused on seclusion and emphasis on meditation. In his memoirs, the Moghul Emperor Jahangir says that 'though they have no religious knowledge or learning of any sort, yet they possess simplicity and are without pretense. They abuse no one. They restrain the tongue of desire and the foot of seeking. They eat no flesh, they have no wives and always plant fruit bearing trees in the fields so that men may benefit by them, themselves desiring no advantage. There are about 2,000 of these people.'

His sayings are preserved in the *Nur-nama*, commonly available in Kashmir. The *Nur-nama* also gives the life of the saint. It was written by Baba Nasib-ud-din Ghazi in Persian about two centuries after the death of Nund Rishi.

He used his poetry as tool to spread the knowledge of the absolute and he vehemently criticized the so-called Mullas and other pseudo-scholars of Islam and gave expression to the lives of the poor and common people of the valleys. He also composed many poems on the pitfalls of the spiritual path and on the love of the devotee for God.

His poetry is commonly known as *Shruks* that are poems in the rhyme structure of A-B, A-B. His shorter 2 couplet *Shruks* of which he composed more than any others are also called, as in the case of the poetry of his mentor Lalleshwari ... *vakhs* that are similar in form and content to the short poems or *sakhis of* the great Kabir who lived at the time of Nund Rishi

His longer poems or *Shruks* are also called *Vatsuns* that have been likened to Persian *ghazals,* the greatest exponent of which, Hafiz of Shiraz, died about 15 years after Nund Rishi was born.

With Lalleshwari (1320-1392), Ghani Kashmiri (d. 1669) and Mahmud Gami (1765-1855) Nund Rishi is considered to be one of the four great Sufi poets of Kashmir.

Selected Bibliography

Lalla to Nuruddin: Rishi-Sufi Poetry of Kashmir, A Translation and Study by Jaishree K.Odin, Motilal Babarsidass Publishers, Delhi, 2013.

A Life of Nans Rishi by Pandit Anand Koul. The Indian Antiquary, 1929, 1930.

Sheikh Noor-ud-din Wali (Nund Rishi) by G.N. Gauhar, Sahitya Akademi, New Delhi, 1988.

Nund Rishi: A Rosary of a Hundred Beads by K.N. Dhar, J & K Academy of Art, Culture & Languages, Srinigar, 1981.

Four Great Sufi Poets of Kashmir: Lalla Ded, Nund Rishi, Ghani Kashmiri & Mahmud Gami, Selected Poems: Translation & Introduction by Paul Smith, New Humanity Books, Campbells Creek, 2016.

Nund Rishi, Life & Poems: Introduction to Sufi Poets Series, Translation & Introduction Paul Smith, New Humanity Books, 2016.

The Book of Lalla Ded (Lalleshwari) Translation & Introduction by Paul Smith, New Humanity Books, Campbells Creek, 2014.

Lalla Ded, Life & Poems, Introduction to Sufi Poets Series, Translation & Introduction Paul Smith, New Humanity Books, 2013.

The Parchment of Kashmir edited by Nyla Ali Khan, Palgrave Macmillan 2012 (pages 71-85).

Kashmir's Transition to Islam: The Role of Muslim Rishis (15th-18th centuries) by M. Ishaq Khan, Manohar Publications 2002.

An Anthology of Kashmiri Verse, Edited by Kh. Hameed Mumtaz, Rawalpindi, 1987.

Gems of Kashmiri Literature by T.N. Kaul, Sanchar Publishing House 1996.

Gems of Kashmiri Literature and Kashmiriyat: The Trio of Sain Poets by P. N. Razdan, Samkaleen Prakashan, New Delhi, 1999.

The Book of Kabir: Translation & Introduction by Paul Smith, New Humanity Books, Campbells Creek, 2013.

Vakhs…

That One is close to me, I to that One:

being near that One I peace discovered.

Outwardly, I wrongly sought the One:

inside I discovered my Friend... indeed!

I, had fallen asleep while I was

awake:

ah no... I feel restless everywhere I

go.

Forbidden I ate, permitted didn't

take:

to temple within with love, I didn't

go.

Hey, you self of mine, listen now carefully:

emptiness news of death goes on creating!

Like sheep to butcher's shop you go finally:

physical body is an illusion, disappearing!

When the bird flies off, the cage stays:

others, will softly weep over the body!

Like a frail flower outer form decays…

O God, of all my sins be forgiving me!

Gold and brass sometimes look similar…

upon seeing this, thinking about it

was I.

Bad I saw grow while the good did suffer:

so then, back into the forest going,

was I.

God inside, is the One I am devoted to...

this 'me' disappearing bit by bit has been.

I'll never be letting go of being devoted to

that One until last door opened has been!

'There is no god, but God' often I did

recite:

then I became absorbed so completely,

in it.

In it I put my heart of stone day and

night...

I was gold from ashes, by being deeply

in it.

That one of Padmanpura, that Lalla...*

nectar by mouthfuls she was drinking.

Everywhere she looked she saw Shiva:

Lord... on me such a gift be bestowing!

*Note: Lalleshwari.

I did ferry the boat across with no oar…
greed and attachment and pride I killed.
With love the Lord I kept on looking for:
my higher Self only then… I recognized.

I'm depending on You, here and

there:

whole of the day I spent, seeking

You!

Absorbed in You as I meditate...

there

I discover bliss inside, because of

You!

Burning up with love is the

lover...

the lover like gold goes on

shining.

The one who is the heart-sick

lover

with the higher Self will be

joining.

That One is there Who is also here:

that One, everywhere can be found.

The chariot and soldier it does bear

is the hidden One, power unbound!

The self leaves if you that One know:

from that One shines such a radiance.

Mind and worry will both quickly go:

from that river who can a sip chance?

You'll be born again if prayers you offer:

cream from milk by praying is separated.

Prayers help in this world and the other:

the door to paradise by praying is parted.

Knowledge is by 'No god but God' saying:

Mohammed follow to walk the path aware.

A year of good acts, pearls up will be piling:

a banquet of devotion, God's path is there!

Truth can be seen as gold in fire

forged:

radiance of illuminated ones is

obvious.

Telling lies is helping illusion to

spread:

sowing seeds that don't sprout,

useless!

You gave honey to be, to man sweetness…

and You gave grapes to the coiling creeper.

Your creation O my Lord, I love to excess!

Deer with musk You trusted as its keeper!

Alif the first letter, means the one

God:

the first to the last... that One is in

all.

Mohammed, is the messenger of

God...

Who'll on Last Day intercede for us

all.

I gave up evil acts for the world I feared:

I devoted my whole life to the only One.

Then in truth's water I my body purified

and I wandered to finally sit in seclusion.

Dearest God... all Your creation, I do adore!

When You know one, that one becomes real!

Dearest Lord, all Your creation, I do adore...

to Prophet miraculous power You did reveal.

Still waters never those pearls will be

containing...

never singing are those birds by cages

bound.

In the piles of ashes daffodils are not

blooming...

at glass-blowers peal-necklaces aren't

found.

Marsh flower's stem is of inferior worth,

the cattle and the horse will it never eat.

When reaching king's head as a wreath...

it's no longer seen as inferior, but a treat.

First is sustenance and then death arrives:

world is like in a city going here and there!

Think of God, on path be one who strives:

listen closely... good and bad actions bear.

Death, is a tiger that one cannot

escape...

like sheep in the flock, you will be

chosen.

Without death's elixir it you'll not

escape:

How is it so early I died way back

then?

Bitter and poisonous and sour and sweet:

that one who bleeding heart is surviving,

whose patience goes on, until complete…

goes to city of the One… there is staying!

Your lower self, do not be abusing…

with your lower self make a bargain

to the ego, lower self, be controlling.

See ego for what it is… God attain!

Some are given duty of fasting and prayer...

God Almighty to them is always generous.

Others spend all their lives wasted in mire:

it is only God Who out, all our fates deals.

Here, there, to some You gave this, that...

here and there the others received nothing.

A necklace of jewels, some received that...

in the light others the dark were receiving.

That One is the first, and the last

too:

go to river's bank... wash off the

impure.

Hands fold up then the One turn

to:

from hell's fire... safety you may

procure.

Flow of the five streams, try to control

by breathing in as deep as you're able!

Your pride with same breath control...

you'll gain the knowledge so valuable.

Meditating, seeking, remembering, considering,

the poison of this lower self I then tossed away.

I held back ego through conscientiously trying...

I thought of the Lord, and gave my home away!

I inhaled one moment, exhaled the next
moment,
my attachment was disappearing,
immediately.
One step became a great distance in a
moment:
my ego, that tiger, was weakened,
immediately.

Hundreds of prayers I offered during the day:
at night I stayed awake, vigil I did maintain.
My prayers may You now accept, this I pray,
if not, O my Lord, like a stay dog I'll remain.

On You I depend, here and there too:

this rose garden make it be blooming.

I gave up all, to now be holding You:

to me You please... be now revealing.

I'm alone but I wish to with my Friend

be:

I want to be each moment with that

One.

Roses are thorns without Friend with

me:

Mecca is where that Friend is, that

One!

At door of that One, one who begins a vigil;

that One offers that one, taste of the nectar.

There are many plays, but one Director still:

whoever's loved by that One becomes a star.

Not hungry and not thirsty, lovers are…

non-lovers for one who never comes wait.

In the oysters the homes of the pearls are:

that thief the ego, sleepless, stays up late.

Realizing the Truth, it couldn't be held in:

Mansur* was burning away… burning up!

A state of peace that one instantly fell in:

not revealed it should have stayed shut up.

*Note: The Perfect Master, poet and martyr Mansur al-Hallaj who was killed for saying, "I am the Truth" (see my 'Mansur Hallaj: Selected Poems' New Humanity Books, 2012).

After they kill the ego those disciplined

are suffering and as servants are acting.

As they use the truth to the One find...

any thing else as ashes, they are seeing.

God's names are many, but… God is

One:

no blade of grass not remembering God

is!

Think of a life of fourteen days in the

sun…

without help of that One not even a fly,

is!

'No god, but God' is source of awareness:

source of good actions is getting ego to go.

That One knows source of Nothingness...

source of the Ocean always flows, no less.

The snow and the ice and icicles too…

all as different God them was making.

In the east the sun rises out of the blue

and the three into the one, are turning!

All those who melt into the inner vision,

on the outside deaf and dumb do appear.

From the fire they come out, no burns on:

for they are priceless gems, to hold dear!

The sower of seeds must endure weeding…
seeking weeds and old branches to remove.
Sower over spring in autumn is weighing…
as a merchant that one heaven will approve.

Clean rust from heart like from a
mirror,
it's how one will come to know the
One.
Your face and form have a young
nature:
die before death, that is knowledge
won!

In the morning angels will be descending,

all those who honour truth they will greet.

All offering others water, stain removing,

there more than here will recognition meet.

They're cut off, as they never stop reading:
into donkeys loaded with books, they turn.
All, who truth in their hearts are knowing
have been blessed with grace… by it learn.

They think they're great, knowledge acquired:

so conceited are those fat ones, O so abusive.

Who from grief into the woods have retreated

will rise though they're now seen as repulsive!

Mullahs cleaned you out and scattered
you:
mullahs, not a bit of knowledge in you I
see!
Mullahs, at the door you lost your way
too:
mullahs... mullahs you don't deserve to
be!

If there was a real mullah, it was Rumi:

if you're not like that one, off to repent!

Rumi was crossing the ocean, where he

received realization of Self. It's evident!

Note: Rumi was the 13th-century Persian poet, jurist, Islamic scholar, theologian, and most importantly Perfect Master and Sufi born in Balkh, Afghanistan in 1207, died in Konya, Turkey 1273. He was the author of 'The Masnavi' & 'Divan of Shams-i Tabriz' and 'Discourses'. Today, he is perhaps the most popular poet in the world. See my 'Book of Rumi' New Humanity Books, 2014 for a large selection of all the types of poems he composed.

By your opinions you are not by God judged,

God judges you... by your spiritual condition.

With tongue stuck on palate remember God:

so that to your trap is drawn the royal swan.

The gross self brings about wanting

the beautiful and the delicious also:

this way, the world and one coming

are lost... for what end did they go?

Vatsuns...

One knows in whom knowledge dawned,

that one God remembers with devotion...

One killing pride, who the ego renounced:

"I'm no one, and I have now not a name!"

Duality leaves one who God experienced:

Who can criticise or complain of that one?

God Almighty is the essence of everything,

and there isn't a moment when this isn't so.

Each quality that One is always enhancing:

that essence does not come and does not go!

To humans highest place that One is giving:

on Self in you concentrate; it's wise to know.

You are nowhere, that One is in each thing:

nightly don't eat or sleep, more aware grow.

Who of this knowledge were never thinking,

day and night in the dark they all blindly go!

I can't say it was dark, that light I witnessed:

I can't say it was nettle, a twig of sweet basil.

Door of this heart of mine, I can't keep closed:

to be soldering gold I can't use glass as the fill.

God, I experienced; I cannot hide it happened:

this self of mine is now that Self and it is, still

I sought God in all worlds, six directions too:

not one trace of that One anywhere did I find.

Mullahs and ascetics I asked, more than two:

I asked many times; they were, less than kind.

When with doubting, thinking, I was through,

that One in all I saw... I was nowhere to find!

Meditation, is to be from hell protected...

meditation, is path the prophets went on.

Meditation means, both worlds are fed...

meditation, is the fragrance to rely upon.

Meditation: if one, is in it, established...

in the two worlds respect is given to one.

All who are spiritually disciplined, who

pray,

are in this world of those who are really

born!

Their plantings are plentiful, sowing all

day:

ripe their harvest is so much more than

corn!

They'll come out of the fire and across

stay...

for it God will reward them and them

adorn!

Like a mad elephant are my desires:

who in reality I am they've crushed.

To my good deeds they've set fires:

caught up... all power from me fled!

One in a thousand from it escapes:

all of the others are soon trampled!

My fair form with the impure is stained...
from this garden the bird has flown away.
Summer's heat into winter's cold changed:
my body has no warmth all night and day!
I have from old age slowly away wasted...
how to I get up, bad actions on me weigh?
Inside I'm black, having the tasty tasted...
I'm so lost, who to ask to help, please say.

My lust is like a poker for hot coals taking,
every moment it's wanting more and more!
Far too weak is mind to of God be thinking:
that I should think of God, I know for sure!
I came into the world as a guest not staying
too long, and now I've lost what I came for!

Whether it is in the cold or in heat too,
always trying hard, practising steadily,
on path lovers sacrifice the self to You
where to flower black bee goes, quickly.
Who this knowledge gets through to…
for such a one, the two are One, to see!

Like filling a chest with gold is knowledge
gaining...

following path is in the agreement to gain
entry.

This agreement isn't really the truth to be
testing...

honesty is a lamp from wind one protects
strongly.

To pray is like to in the earth the seeds be
sowing...

with reverence, that is fine, they will ripen
evenly.

The heart is like a fish... so do not let it be
drying:

by remembering God water it... it will be
lovely.

The self is a real gem, and so it do not be
losing...

the Beloved is God, and that One will be
happy!

When God appeared to those much loved,

the One appeared in a vision to Mansur.*

On love's wine, he was made intoxicated,

God… had others, him like a thief murder.

When with musk, saffron, he was purified,

his heart filled with bliss at the open door.

*Note: Mansur Hallaj (d.919 A.D.), who was sentenced to death for saying:
"I am the Truth (Anal Haq)." Much has been written about Hallaj and his
famous (and infamous statement. On Mansur Hallaj's life and sayings and
his poems see my: 'The Book of Mansur al-Hallaj' New Humanity Books
2014.

Real knowledge is coming from what
with love, one's true nature is filling.
If form's pure and calm and the heart
is one, it in faith guidance is seeking.
Confusion will disappear when that
duality goes: One, is then revealing.

Adam's nature was made from earth by God,

that one's form, was shaped out of the clay...

from clay, God every thing in nature created;

cooking now happens in pots made from clay.

The body goes back to clay, if life's departed:

clay's then again mixed with even more clay!

A scholar spins out words that are sweet…

down that face the beads keep on trickling.

That one has a stack of books near to feet…

looking inside he at last is animated thing.

We see he is nothing inside, is incomplete:

forgets who he is, when others criticising!

Some have closed eyes but aren't sleeping:
some are shut off because they're ignorant.
Some in fire of love are burning, burning...
some are ashes and others gold to enchant.
Some before their death away are dying...
they turn from ashes to gold, a rare event!

First Rishi was Mohammed Rishi:[*]

second, Uways Qarani[*] following.

The third Rishi, was Zalak Rishi…

the fourth Hazrat Palas, following.

The fifth Rishi was Rumai Rishi…

the sixth Hazrat Miran, following.

Seventh never as advanced was he:

I'm no one and my name's nothing!

*Notes: Mohammed is Prophet Mohammed, whom many see as the first Sufi (Rishi in Kashmir) of the time. *Uways Qarani, from Yemen, was a Perfect Master at the time of Prophet Mohammed, who didn't need to see Mohammed to accept him as the Divine Prophet. In honour of Mohammed who had lost his teeth in the battle of Ohod, Uways pulled out his own teeth. Mohammed said of Uways: "Truly, from the quarters of Yemen, I perceive the perfume of God." A form of Sufism was named after him as it refers to the transmission of spiritual knowledge between two individuals without need for physical interaction between them. All the other Spiritual Masters mentioned are unknown.

When God was proudly Adam naming,

God was filling up that one, with mercy.

I am joyful, whether I am dead or living:

that One's my Lord and I serve humbly.

The One earth and sky was beautifying:

to faithful was sent apostle trustworthy.

I hold out hope I'll eventually be rising...

my Guide here remains Uways Qarani.*

*Note: Uways Qarani: see previous note.

Self-pity lose… hardship be welcoming:
go… and live on wild herbs and chicory!
Give up pride, moderation be following:
put up with grief; then, you'll be happy.
Abandon greed, to be good keep trying:
crossing river of world, force self to be!

At times by boat you go, or by foot go...

if you're confused you'll not get through!

But, if you steadfast along one path go...

the distant goal will not be worrying you.

Until world's chains you make let you go

you will find contentment is far off... too.

Some the divine call were

receiving,

others make a great effort for

grace.

Some the divine wine were

drinking:

some, the locusts ate out their

place.

Some from destitution were

leaving:

others lost things, shops, not a

trace!

Master's guidance is pears and sugar...
that is, if it you're accepting and loving.
Ask for blessing when with the Master
so that your heart will find it... calming.
All confusion in the mind will disappear
and only that One you'll be discovering.

Don't go on and on rubbing your body,

the soap will never it be truly cleaning.

Beads, staff, robe… patched, carefully:

tricks won't you to the One be leading.

Give up all desires and a servant be…

you will then know, the true teaching!

Ashamed you will be there eventually:

here and there… is only the one Being.

Be humble and go looking for safety…

right way take, wrong don't be going!

One purifying five senses completely

will see in heart and is bliss knowing.

We were sent into this world by the One

and through faith we have a relationship.

We were given horses, whips by the One:

we ride form… control with mind's whip.

If for that One we die, all… we have won!

The One's so near to us, no need of a trip.

Riches and land, a house with a balcony:

to desire the world a lot is... undesirable!

Give up, it's no way to gain spirituality:

think of God day and night, be spiritual!

Be fearful of criticism from the divinity...

so you do not do actions that are hurtful.

One who goes into a forest into seclusion,

accepting pain, to truth is totally devoted:

one who is patient and eats in moderation

who sees one's self as nothing as finished;

in that solitude thinks about own oblivion:

such a one as a 'Muslim' should be called.

I see you, body, like you were far away:

you from the forest into the field went.

Young, you as a robber, went astray...

that robber is really mind... is evident.

If to God you'd honestly found a way

as king of all six you'd them off sent. *

*Note: The six are the five senses and the mind. The poet was a robber in his youth.

Printed in Great Britain
by Amazon

32555246R00150